C

poems by
FRED CHAPPELL

LOUISIANA STATE UNIVERSITY PRESS
Baton Rouge and London

1993

02 01 00 99 98 97 96 95 94 93   5 4 3 2 1

Designer: Glynnis Phoebe
Typeface: Bembo
Typesetter: G & S Typesetters, Inc.
Printer and binder: Thomson-Shore, Inc.

Library of Congress Cataloging-in-Publication Data
Chappell, Fred, 1936–
    C : poems / by Fred Chappell.
       p.   cm.
    ISBN 0-8071-1784-6 (alk. paper).—ISBN 0-8071-1785-4 (pbk. :
alk. paper)
    I. Title.
PS3553.H298C23   1993
811'.54—dc20
                                                                    92-28214
                                                                    CIP

The following poems appeared originally in the publications indicated: in *Chronicles,*
"Malgré Lui" (XIII), "The Epigrammatist" (C), "Literary Critic" (XXIII), "Another"
(XXIV), "Another" (XXV), "Another" (XXVI), "Another" (XXVII), "Another"
(XVIII), "Another" (XXIX); in the *Chronicle of Higher Education,* "The Stories" (LXIII);
in *Colonnades,* "The Intimation" (XL); in *College English,* "A Glorious Twilight"
(LXI); in the *Davidson Miscellany,* "The Old Actor" (LXXX); in the *Formalist,* "Ave
atque Vale" (LVIII), "Upon a Confessional Poet" (XV); in the Greensboro *Sun,* "Daisy"
(VIII), "White Clover" (IX), "Chipmunk" (X), "Toadstool" (XIX), "Dandelion"
(XXI), "Nettle" (XLVI); in *Hardscrabble,* "Dressage" (XLVIII); in *Hemlocks & Balsams,*
"Upon a Municipal Architect" (XXXVII), "Epitaph: Lydia" (LIV), "Sex Manual" (LV);
in *International Poetry Review,* "Depot" (LXXI), "The Swallows" (LXXII), "2 in 1"
(LXXIII), "Gigi" (LXXIV), "What Fun:" (LXXV), "Now Look Here" (LXXVI); in
New Virginia Review, "In the Garden" (LXXXIX); in *Poultry,* "The Ubi Sunt Lament of
the Beldame Hen" (LXXXIV); in the *Sow's Ear,* "Morning Light" (IV), "L'Amoureuse"
(LVI), "Allora" (LXX), "Threads" (LXXVII), "First Novel" (XIV), "A Reflection"
(XCV); in *Tar Heel,* "Honeysuckle" (XX).

Publication of this book has been supported by a grant from the National Endowment
for the Arts in Washington, D.C., a federal agency.

In memoriam:
Douglas Minyard

CONTENTS

C

I PROEM

In such a book as this,
The poet Martial says,
Some of the epigrams
Shall have seen better days,
And some are hit-or-miss;
But some—like telegrams—
Deliver intelligence
With such a sudden blaze
The shine can make us wince.

II   SMALL IS BEAUTIFUL

You've told me, Gaurus, I have little art
Because I make my teasing poems short.
But then am I to think your genius soars
Because you write twelve tomes of Priam's wars?
To carve a statuette is my hard duty.
You heap a bloat colossus of Silly Putty.

—Martial

III   SATIRE

Not to write satire is hard,
Said Juvenal. But the ancient chorus
Is silenced; Aristophanes
And Terence now go quite unheard,
Their lines too moderate to please:
The morning headlines write our satire for us.

IV   MORNING LIGHT

Immensity
Illumes me.

—Giuseppe Ungaretti

V HOW TO DO IT

"Chappell—you who love to jest—
Hear the things that make life blest:
Family money not got by earning;
A fertile farm, a hearthfire burning;
No lawsuits and no formal dress;
A healthy body and a mind at peace;
Friends whom tactful frankness pleases;
Good meals without exotic sauces;
Sober nights that still spark life;
A faithful yet a sexy wife;
Sleep that makes the darkness brief;
Contentment with what you plainly need;
A death not longed for, but without dread."
                                        —*Martial*

VI REJOINDER

Now let's even up the score
And tell what things make life a bore:
Sappy girls who kiss and tell;
Televangelists' threats of hell;
Whining chain saws, mating cats;
Republicans; and Democrats;
Expertly tearful on their knees,
Plushlined senators copping pleas,
Swearing by the Rock of Ages
That they did not molest their pages;
Insurance forms and tax reports;
Flabby jokes and lame retorts;
Do-gooders, jocks, and feminists;
Poems that are merely lists.

3

VII AUBADE

Wake up, Susan. Let's walk around the lake
This morning while the air is cool and rain
Drips from the oaks after the midnight storm.
The day coming on will be fuzzy-warm,
Too muggy for a comfortable hike.
This freshened hour will not come again.

Perhaps you'd choose to walk down by the bog
To see the ducklings paddle as the sun
Rays through the trees to burn away the fog
Rising off the water still night-cool,
And watch the heron grooming on her log—
And never see another human soul.

VIII   DAISY

> Men build Parises and Zions;
> I, wide meadows of Orions.
> Rome took two thousand years, but in one day
> I built a Milky Way.

IX   WHITE CLOVER

> So many votes of Yea
> We place in tally
> That on a summer day
> In the grass-green valley
> Our broad democracy
> Shines like the sea.

X   CHIPMUNK

> Don't blink, or
> I'm gone,
> Slow thinker.

XI   EPITAPH: THE POET

I never truckled.
I never pandered.
I was born
To be remaindered.

XII   EPITAPH: THE REPROBATE

I truckled and I pandered
And also lied and slandered
And rioted and squandered
And died at age one hundred
A stranger unafraid
In a bed I never made.

XIII   MALGRÉ LUI

Jerry earns his bread writing polemics
Against the footnote race of academics.
Pompous, he calls them, *ineffectual
Officious pedants,* and so forth. Why
Does he so complain and vilify?
—Don't breathe this secret to a living soul:
Jerry's a latent intellectual.

XIV FIRST NOVEL

And then in April the old priest died.
Your mother, the letter said. *Come soon.*
The blonde girl looked at him and sighed.
Over the silent lake the moon.

"I love only you," said the doctor's wife.
They were struggling for the pistol when
He suddenly realized that his life.
It rained in Paris next day again.

XV UPON A CONFESSIONAL POET

You've shown us all in stark undress
The sins you needed to confess.
If my peccadilloes were so small
I never would undress at all.

XVI REBELLIOUS CHILD

He treasures up their insults,
Counts the belt-blows one by one.
They read in bitter eyes the truth:
He knows what they've done.

XVII   NO DEFENSE

" 'Even Homer nods,' you said;
    You've said it many times before.
    It won't apply in your case, Fred.
    He doesn't pass out cold and snore."

XVIII   CONSENSUS

You've purchased a table for five thousand dollars;
        "It's really quite a bargain," you say.
So you and I and our friends all agree.
Each of us knows that you'll never pay.

                                        —*Martial*

XIX   TOADSTOOL

He's the oddest fellow
    Ever was made,
Lifting his white umbrella
    To ward off shade.

XX   HONEYSUCKLE

Granted by right divine,
I say, *this field is mine!*

XXI   DANDELION

Ponder, friend, in me
    Mortality.
Even the yellow sun
Dwindles from the One,
    Grows old and gray.
And the clock blows away.

XXII   DODDER

Lord, list me not
Among Thy negatives.
Everything that lives
Upon this little spot
Of Earth believes.
          Believes.

XXIII LITERARY CRITIC

Blandword died, and now his ghost
Drifts gray through lobby, office, hall.
Some mourn diminished presence; most
Can see no difference at all.

XXIV ANOTHER

Dr. Cheynesaugh has one rule
That makes all others void and null,
Embodying this sentiment:
Guilty till proven innocent.

XXV ANOTHER

Professor Pliant flits from school to school.
An Archetypal Marxian Feminist,
A faithful Structural Deconstructionist,
His beige enthusiasms never cool.

And never warm. As any führer's disciple
He finds himself unable to confute or
Challenge the weakest intellectual cripple.
He is the very model of a hermeneuter.

XXVI ANOTHER

Blossom's footnotes never shirk
The task of touting his own work.

XXVII ANOTHER

Peter Puffer piped a pack of poets into
Undeservedly prominent public view;
Then, just to prove the power of his pen,
Provokingly piped them pouting out again.

XXVIII ANOTHER

Strychnine writes impartially
Of novels, plays, and poetry;
His judgements upon authors are
By his own lights impeccably fair
Because when all is said and done
By God he hates them every one.

XXIX ANOTHER

Procrustes kept a Theory as a pet
And fed it all the verses he could get.
One day it swallowed down a bona fide
Poem, fell ill, turned blue, and died.
He got it stuffed and keeps it on display,
Pleased to see it worshipped every day.

XXX   REPLY LETTER

Please excuse the pages ripped,
Stranger, in your manuscript,
Places where my pencil tore
Through two sheets and sometimes more.
I've marked some passages so red
They must look as if they'd bled;
And when you see my savage scratches
Setting off your purple patches,
You'll think your book has had a fight
In a pool hall Saturday night.
But that's not true, for I've admired
The way you get my passions fired.
Please understand: I here present
The sincerest form of compliment.

XXXI   TELEVANGELIST

He claims that he'll reign equally
With Jesus in eternity.
But it's not like him to be willing
To give a partner equal billing.

XXXII   OVERHEARD IN THE
TEAROOM

"Marianne, my dear,
I'll say this for Ruth:
Though she never tells the truth
Her lies are quite sincere."

XXXIII   GRACE BEFORE MEAT

As this noon our meat we carve,
Bless us better than we deserve.

XXXIV   ANOTHER

Bless, O Lord, our daily bread.
Bless those in hunger and in need
Of strength. Bless all who stand in want.
Bless us who pray, bless us who can't.

XXXV   ANOTHER

Bless our corn pones, Lord. But let us dream
They might be black currant muffins with strawberry
jam and clotted double Devon cream.

XXXVI   AGRICULTURE

You've planted seven wealthy husbands
    While the bodies were still warm.
You own, Chloë, what I'd call
    A profit-making farm.
                            —*Martial*

XXXVII   UPON A MUNICIPAL ARCHITECT

Such forts he builds you'd think the enemy
    Was quite upon us, and no cavalry
To ride to our rescue. Why does he shape
These beetling heaps that say: *Abandon hope
    All ye who enter here?* Does he predict
    Taxpayers rising up in armed conflict
Against these concrete horrors? Does he decide
They'll be the safest places he can hide?
Then he deceives himself. For even now
They melt like bonbons pissed on by a cow.

XXXVIII   SNOWFLAKE

What fine designs you have upon us,
        O Sugar-star!

XXXIX   A FIELD OF ORCHARD GRASS

Feminfinite sea, wavelight breaking
on the afternoon like the silence of harps.
                                    —*Max Albern*

XL   THE INTIMATION

August departs the hill
In a thunder of butterflies.
Evanishment of forefathers, blue wide salver
Of sky presents the slow-settling dust.
The Summer is walking away,
Leaving its footprints in flesh.
                                    —*Max Albern*

XLI   R X

Dr. Rigsbee
Drank all my whiskey.
He said, when I objected, "Hell,
Fred, you're paying me to make you well."
                              —*Martial*

XLII   THE TRUTH AT LAST

I do not love thee, Dr. Fell;
The reason why I'm going to tell
Although your lawyers threaten suit.

For I'm too sick to give a hoot.

XLIII   FORESHADOWING

Never ill a single hour,
    Why did Crispus die?
Because he dreamed that he'd been treated
    By Dr. Slye.

—Lucilius

XLIV   MEMORIAL

In the plaza Dr. Shaddoe
Found the memorial to General Hyde.
Where he touched, the stone turned black.
Two weeks later the statue died.

—Ausonius

XLV FOR THE TOMB OF THE LITTLE DOG ZABOT

Your house was small, your body but a puplet;
A shoebox was your grave, your epitaph this couplet.
                                              —*Petrarch*

XLVI NETTLE

I have teeth
Beneath;
And a flower too
Of cool blue
With a center star
Of yellow sheath.

As common as air,
Startling as fire.

XLVII   MARIGOLD

Daystar crinkled
Upon the stream,
Flower of sultry dream
Where the bee twinkled.

XLVIII   DRESSAGE

The discipline is
to make her believe she thinks,
that she turn cooly to your gesture
the way the leaves of the poplar sapling
touch the wind.

Yet it must be unseen,
invisible as the will.

You are her eyes, she has become your hands.

XLIX   A WOMAN

Of Felicity
Impossible to say if she is flesh or
Fantasy:
The kind of woman who gives money pleasure.

L   ANOTHER

What kind of girl do I prefer?
Flaccus wants to know. Not her
Who acquiesces the first hour,
Nor her who stays forever dour.
I like her when it's just enough:
Neither a girl who puts me on,
Nor one who puts me off.
                              —Martial

LI   EPITAPH: THE PLAYBOY

It was wine and women
That did me in.
If I get a chance
They'll do it again.

LII   BLUE LAW

Dancing girls, take off your clothes.
Lend spirit to our dwindling hours—
For Spirit will at last disclose
The full enormity of its powers,
Denuding the dull Hypocrisies
Who force their G-strings on the flowers.

LIII   EL PERFECTO

Senator No sets up as referee
Of everything we read and think and see.
His justification for such stiff decreeing
Is being born a perfect human being
Without a jot of blemish, taint, or flaw,
The Dixie embodiment of Moral Law,
Quite fit and eager to pursue the quarrel
With God Whose handiwork he finds immoral.

LIV   EPITAPH: LYDIA

She enjoyed making love
In any exotic location.
Now Lydia lies here.
It's not the first occasion.

LV   SEX MANUAL

We've followed instructions to the letter,
Pausing at diagram 82.
"Aren't we there yet?" one of us queries.
But in this position I can't tell who.

LVI L'AMOUREUSE

Upon my eyelids she stands
And her hair is mingled with mine;
She has the shape of my hands,
She has the color of my eyes;
In my shadow she is swallowed
Like a stone against the skies.

Her eyes are open always,
And so I cannot sleep.
Her dreams in full daylight
Evaporate the suns
And make me laugh and make me cry
And babble babble thoughtlessly.
                              —Paul Éluard

LVII   THE VOICE

Love had placed his sign upon her face,
And she so took my heart, this wanderer,
That other women seemed to lack all grace.

And through the new green grass I followed her
Until I heard a voice from a distant height:
"In this wood all paths lose themselves. Beware."

Then in the shadow of a grand beech tree
I took shelter, engrossed in thought, and soon
I saw what forward dangers threatened me—

And turned back home almost exact at noon.

—Petrarch

LVIII   AVE ATQUE VALE

Weeping, I mended the broken wing
Of Love and calmed his shuddering
And bound his wounded hand and then
I watched him fly away again.

LIX   I LOVE YOU

Yet you were gone six days before
I took from the bedroom closet the dress,
The blue and white one that you wore
To that dinner party that was such a mess,
And fearfully hung it on the door
And sat before it in a chair,
Remembering what and when and where,
And touched it with a ghost's caress.

LX MIDWAY IN THIS LIFE

The landscape in the lake
all hung with yellow pears
and overwhelmed with wild roses:

O lovely swans
drunk with kisses,
plunge your heads
into this water lucid and supernal.

But as for me,
where shall I gather in wintertime
the flowers, where
the sunshine and shadows of the earth?
The battlements stand mute and cold.
In the wind
the pennons chirr.

—Hölderlin

LXI   A GLORIOUS TWILIGHT

Susan is painting her nails
such a brilliant shade of bright
she seems to have sprouted 22 fingers

Don't need open-toed shoes, those toes
would gleam through blind galoshes
like designer Northern Lights

Be careful, I said, waving your phalanges about!
You're gonna burn the house down

And then the house began to bulge
With the light of fingernails
And lifted through the air
Through clouds where it snows and hails
And came to rest beside
The pale-by-comparison moon
And glowed on the earnest astronomer
Like a Passion Fire doubloon

LXII   WEDDING ANNIVERSARY

Gale winds tore this tree
And drought and frost came near
To killing it. But see:
In its thirtieth year
It blooms like a candleflame,
And puts its youth to shame.

LXIII   THE STORIES

The story of lovers torn apart by war is a thousand
    pages long.

The story of lovers whom money separates fills all
    the stiff ledgers of Europe.

By the light of a single candle I read the tale of
    lovers grown old together, climbing faithfully
    to the darkened landing of the stairway.

LXIV   COMING HOME

Even the sunlight is a smell you remembered.

LXV   A HANGING LAMP

In the salon-hall silent and disused,
An elegant chain suspends, as if it floated,
An antique lamp with its white marble bowl.
An ivy wreath around the rim is enchased
In green-gold bronze; carven children hurtle
And laugh, a Ring Around the Rosy circle.
A playful serious purpose informs the whole
Of this fine work left here where no one sees:
Perfect radiance of self-sufficiencies.
                                    —*Mörike*

LXVI   DEFINITION

The only animal that dares to play the bagpipes.

LXVII   COROLLARY

Or wants to.

LXVIII EPITAPH: PREVARICATION

A lonely sorrow
This monument tells:
Here lies one
Who did nothing else.

LXIX   THE STARS

The stars look down to see

in the slaughterhouse by the moaning pens
Earth gone down on her knees
to service the drunken colonel and the briber of colonels

The stars avert their eyes and flee away

In the sierra then
the final puma looks up to find
the stars departed
and the night all black

LXX ALLORA

The good old days . . . Once upon
A time I went my happy ways.
Not now, but I remember when
And feel the spell of the good old days.

Oh, what a year that was! The years
That since have fled, that yet shall flee,
I cannot find within my powers
To hold in equal memory.

There was an hour without a peer.
Never shall it return again.
After that hour and ever before
All my hours were false and vain.

A moment only! And it was gone.
It was beautiful to me
And yet so fleet I had never known.
But I was happy unbearably.
                              —*Giovanni Pascoli*

SIX POEMS BY "FARFA"

LXXI DEPOT

look. how the arched roof,
the gypsy girl's mouth
is blowing cigar smoke:
train heading out

and now she pokes it
once more between her lips:
here comes the super express

just as far as you can spit
the last little butt:
goodbye caboose

LXXII THE SWALLOWS

in nifty capitals of black satin
they're typing out the aubade
daybreak just dictated

LXXIII 2 IN 1

if I could steal into the strands
of your blonde hair
I know for a fact my blood
would change color, would turn
pure gold

LXXIV   GIGI

I'm queasy this evening
bring me one of those 7-colored
cocktails like they drink in Paris
I wanna go somewhere over the rainbow

LXXV   WHAT FUN:

to see how the gasping train
climbs the ladder of rail ties
to get to the mouth of the tunnel
and be sucked in like a licorice stick

LXXVI   NOW LOOK HERE

listen little abbess
hunched over behind the lattice
like you were at early prayers
gimme my goddam TICKET

this ain't
no station of the cross

it's the Turin
TRAIN station
        —(*Vittorio Tommasini*)

LXXVII   THREADS

Listen, buddy, I knew you when
You were a man like other men,
Not on your high horse, puffed with pride,
But genial, friendly, bona fide.

Now you think you're a different breed
Because you wear expensive tweed
And flash the label that declares it.

But a sheep first wore it. A sheep still wears it.
                                    —*Buchanan*

LXXVIII   STAND-UP COMIC

Grimacing, sweating, he shrieks obscenities,
    Bellows his punch lines again and again,
Until we ask ourselves what kind of mirth
    Could cause a man such tearing pain.

LXXIX   UPON AN AMOROUS OLD COUPLE

This coltish April weather
Has caused them to aspire
To rub dry sticks together
In hopes that they'll catch fire.

LXXX   THE OLD ACTOR

A palimpsest.
Death, to reach him with a final cue,
must strip away eleven
Hamlets, twenty years' Othellos,
a stiff-necked Lear or two, layer
on layer of Restoration polish,
a variorum of bowing servitors,
attendants, and broad-voweled nobility.
Beyond the callow Romeo
there stands at last a man, the best parts
of him absent.

He takes the slip
that Grinning Mask proffers; reads;
starts back in staring horror.
Ad libitum he strikes his heart.
Is This, Then, All? He crumples Alas
majestically, as waves like thundering
applause break over a floodlit shore.

LXXXI   LIBERAL

Faced with the problem of Original Sin,
He applies to Science for a sure vaccine.

LXXXII   CONSERVATIVE

He trudges Main Street into a murky rut,
And thinks such normal thoughts that he's a nut.

LXXXIII VILLON

I'm François from the district of Pontoise,
    Poet, thief, and human wreck.
    An hour from now they hang my ass
Just to test the muscles of my neck.
                    —Rabelais

LXXXIV THE UBI SUNT LAMENT OF THE BELDAME HEN

Is there no one who can tell
The tales of heroes of the olden days,
Their voices strong as the chapel bell?
When they strutted their stuff on straw runways
Their plumage shed resplendent rays.
O where is noble Chanticleer
On whom the world adored to gaze?
Where are the cocks of yesteryear?

There was a rooster journeyed to hell,
Or so the ancient legend says,
Who conquered there and came back whole,
To fill the world with strange amaze.
O Orpheus, in limp times like these
We need a champion who has no fear
To shame the devil to his face.
But where are the cocks of yesteryear?

Where are Gawain and William Tell,
Veterans of a thousand frays?
Where is Ajax who never fell,
And had such polish, such winning grace,
He was the jewel of our race?
With eye so red and comb so rare,
His was the look that truly slays.
O where are the cocks of yesteryear?

This conundrum that I raise
Was broached of old by La Belle Heaulmière
In Master Villon's langue française:
Where are the cocks of yesteryear?

LXXXV   EPITAPH: JUSTICE

The poet Hipponax lies here.
In justice, this is only fair.
His lines were never dark or deep.
Now he enjoys (like his readers) sleep.
                            —*Theocritus*

LXXXVI   A RIDDLE

However still and dark the night
For the soldier it is light;
When the silent stars abound
For the guiltless it is sound;
While days and years their vigils keep
In the graveyard it is deep.

(*sleep*)

LXXXVII   ANOTHER

It glazed the crackling fallen leaves
And hung long daggers from the eaves,
Transformed every power line
Into a streak of silver shine,
And made each heavy tree appear
A tinkling crystal chandelier.

Then as morning climbed toward noon,
It all came gaily crashing down.

(*ice storm*)

LXXXVIII   ANOTHER

Nobody knows
How fast it goes
Until he shows
That where it is
Is not a tease
Of appearances.

To do this deed
He changes the speed
Of the object there—
(What object? Where?)—
Making unknown
What he had shown
To be truly so
A moment ago.

*(Heisenberg's
Uncertainty Principle)*

LXXXIX IN THE GARDEN

The guitar's rubato quivered
And died. The woman shivered
And lifted toward the night her head.
He set his wine glass on the tray.
There was something fragile they had feared to say.
Now it was said.

XC   SERENADE

Let's stay at home tonight and build a fire
And turn the television off and read
And play some Haydn on the record player.
Maybe we'll bake a lemon gingerbread
To eat with coffee-and-Kahlúa. I know
You know the weather forecast calls for snow.

While I was walking back I saw the light
Mass thick with cloud and felt the cutlass wind
Swipe down from the north, shaking the beeches
Like corn tassels. Along the smeary reaches
Southward the sky went yellow as river sand.
That's when I thought: "Let's stay at home tonight."

XCI BEDTIME PRAYER

Lord, hold us safe until daybreak
While moon and stars their motions take
And let us be all for Thy sake
If we sleep or if we wake.

XCII ANOTHER

Now the night has come again,
Keep us safely in Your thought;
And when the day begins to shine
Help us do the things we ought.

XCIII ANOTHER

Now the day is at an end.
In the night be Thou my Friend.

XCIV   AUTUMN OAKS

Our trees, those brides, are stripping now to skeletons.
And so shall I when I am wed to Winter.
—*Max Albern*

XCV   A REFLECTION

All day sunward raged the thirst
Of mankind, and the anguished groan.

Midnight now. The still lake proffers
Its blind communion wafer moon.

XCVI   THE MOON REGARDS THE
        FROZEN EARTH

Have you, my sister, done at last
With your green and foolish frippery,
Deciding that bone white is best
For wedding proud Eternity?

So I decided long ago.
And I must say, *I told you so*.

XCVII   THE EARTH REPLIES

This Fimbul Winter that mantles me
Is not my wedding finery.
It is my silver winding-sheet.
Now that the sun has banked his heat,
Closing down with a tremulous wink,
We worlds who once were fat with grass
Clink like ice cubes in a glass,
Although the party's over.
                          Still,
I've known things you never will,
And in the long silence to come
I'll have seasons on which to dream.

XCVIII   TO OLD AGE

Long have we lived together, Friend,
Peaceably, amicably.
Not that this state of things should end,
But if there's someone who'll receive
You with warmer hospitality,
You have my glad consent to leave.
                              —Landor